This dood

_____

Your name

_____

Date

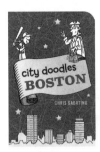

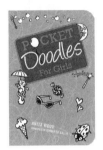
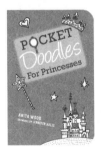

city doodles
NEW YORK

BILL ZIMMERMAN
DRAWINGS BY **TOM BLOOM**

GIBBS SMITH
TO ENRICH AND INSPIRE HUMANKIND

For my wife, who loves to ride the buses in New York
and knows all the routes. She always encourages
and inspires me with her enthusiasm for life.
—BZ

To KR, JB, MBLM & NYC. XOX.
—TB

Manufactured in Altona, Manitoba, Canada
in January 2013 by Friesen

First Edition
17 16 15 14 13   5 4 3 2 1

Text © 2013 Bill Zimmerman
Illustrations © 2013 Tom Bloom

Published by
Gibbs Smith
P.O. Box 667
Layton, Utah 84041

1.800.835.4993 orders
www.gibbs-smith.com

Designed by Melissa Dymock and Renee Bond

Gibbs Smith books are printed on either recycled, 100%
post-consumer waste, FSC-certified papers or on paper
produced from sustainable PEFC-certified forest/
controlled wood source. Learn more at www.pefc.org.

ISBN 13: 978-1-4236-3227-6

Dear Reader,

My great love affair with New York began when I was a boy growing up in Brooklyn. The most exciting times were those Saturdays when my father took me to work with him on the elevated train from Brooklyn to the city (Manhattan), where he worked as a furrier in the fur district. There, he showed me how he made fur coats, and later in the day he'd take me for lunch, either to a Jewish delicatessen or an Italian restaurant. So delicious!

Other early New York memories revolve around those special days, such as my birthday or Easter, when my mother would take my brother and me to the city to see a movie and stage show at Radio City Music Hall, with the famous dancing Rockettes, or to the Broadway theatre district to see a musical comedy.

My eyes would open up like saucers when I walked in the city then, excited by its spectacular sights, its streets teeming with people. As young as I was, I knew back then that this was where the action was and I wanted to be part of it. Looking up, up, up at the towering skyscrapers I'd imagine the day when I was grown up and working on the highest floors of one of these buildings—I wanted an office in the sky. With time my dream did come true: after graduating from a free city college I got a job and moved to Manhattan. I became a newspaper editor and finally achieved that big office overlooking the city and the Hudson River.

Over the years I have traveled to major cities throughout the United States and the world, but as wonderful as these places were, they never topped New York as a city of endless fascination and possibilities. In this playful doodling book, my artist friend Tom Bloom and I have tried to share with you all the things we love about New York, a city with five different boroughs, with so many different sights and neighborhoods and a wide range of people.

As you doodle, draw, write and color in this book, no matter what town or country you live in, you will be "walking" with us through the streets of New York, experiencing its richness and life. You see, to me New York City is like a great toy chest that you can open up daily and always discover some new treasure. May you never be bored and always have adventures with our book. Come visit!

Sincerely,

Bill Zimmerman

Bill Zimmerman

Add some lights and ornaments to the giant Christmas tree at Rockefeller Center.

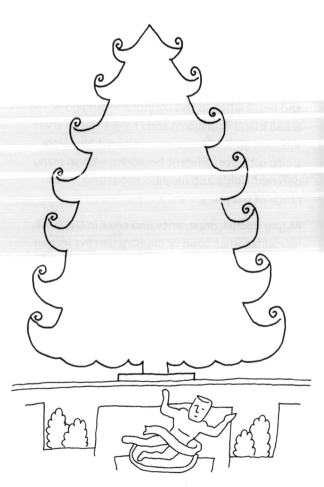

What do you see from the deck of the Staten Island Ferry?

Doodle what these sightseers see from the top of this double-decker bus.

What does this boy see from the top of the Empire State Building?

Draw the steeple for the art deco-style Chrysler Building.

Add the tops on these New York City skyscrapers.

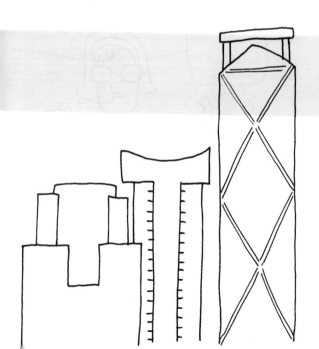

What are this woman and her hungry pigeon friends thinking?

Draw some of the fantastic costumes seen at the annual Halloween Parade in Greenwich Village.

What kind of parade would *you* like to see in New York? Finish drawing the signs.

Design a new baseball uniform
for the New York Yankees.

Who's waiting for the subway train? Finish doodling the people on the platform.

Design some eye-catching clothes on the runway at New York Fashion Week.

Your film is being shown at the New York Film Festival. What's it called?

Practice, practice, practice got him to Carnegie Hall. Finish drawing the musician and his instrument.

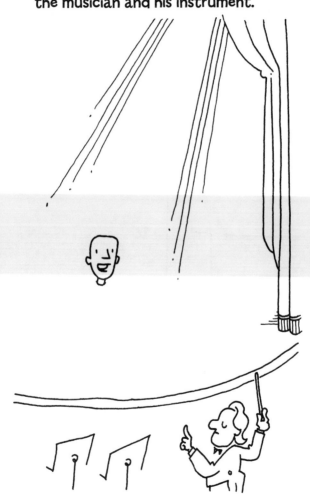

How many things can you do in a "New York minute"? Make a list.

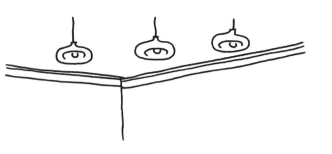

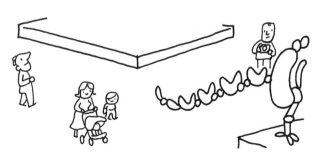

Add a dinosaur to this exhibit at the American Museum of Natural History.

Add some buildings to the
New York skyline.

Draw some fireworks over the
Hudson River for the annual Fourth
of July fireworks celebration.

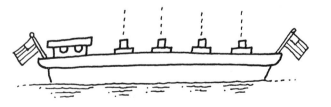

What are this dog walker and his four-footed friends thinking?

Design a giant new balloon
for the annual Macy's
Thanksgiving Day Parade.

Draw some stars and constellations at the Hayden Planetarium Space Show.

Add some vivid neon signs and lights to the buildings in Times Square.

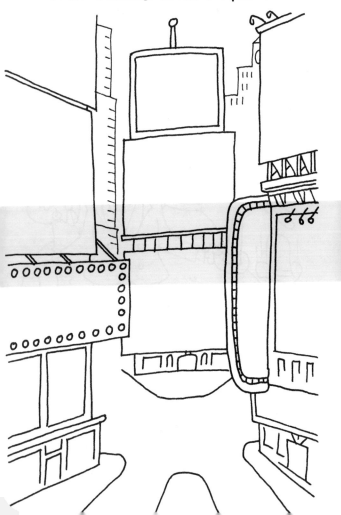

Draw some odd hats for these people gathered around the Mad Hatter on the *Alice in Wonderland* statue in Central Park.

Connect these lines and shapes to design a new skyscraper.

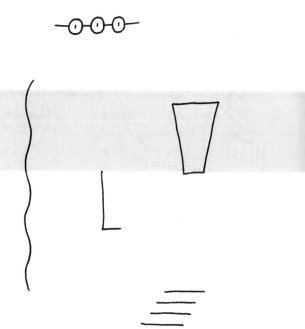

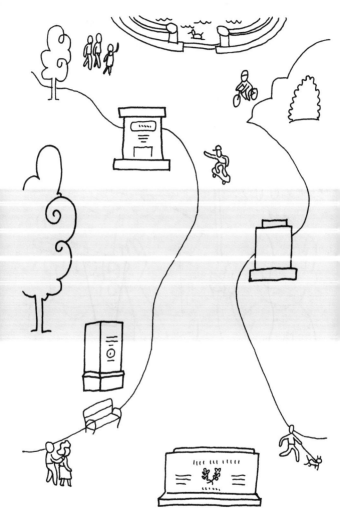

Add some new statues in Central Park.

Doodle some designs on the T-shirts for sale in the Big Apple Souvenir Shop.

Draw some trendy clothes for these
fashion design students at the
Fashion Institute of Technology.

Students at the New York Institute of Technology have come up with some new game for your tablet. What does it do?

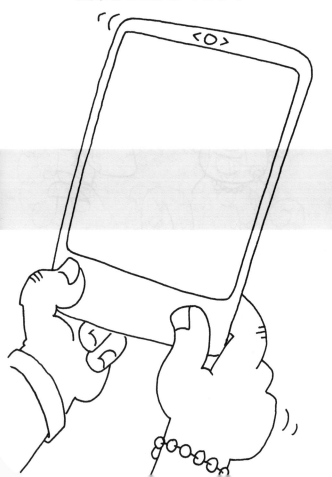

Draw some outrageous hats for the Easter Parade on Fifth Avenue.

Doodle some graffiti on the
sides of these subway trains.

What is this street vendor selling?

What are this customer and server at Katz's Deli on Manhattan's Lower East Side saying?

Your Observations. Doodle or write about New York City.

What show is playing on Broadway that you'd like to see?

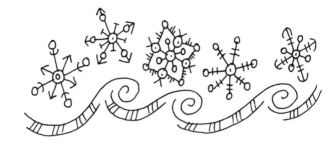

Add some more dancers to this line of
Rockettes at Radio City Music Hall.

The State of Liberty is missing her torch. Draw it.

Draw someone you saw in SoHo.

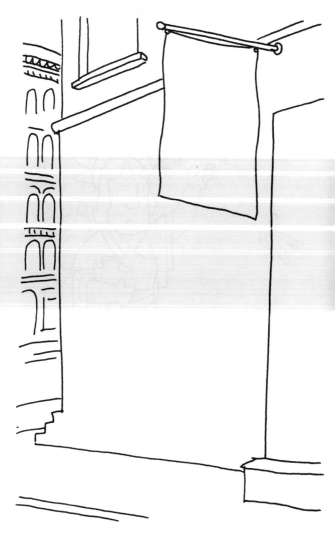

This is what the sophisticated New Yorker is wearing.

Write or draw the strangest sight
you saw today in New York City.

Build a sand castle at Coney Island.

The circus has come to New York.
Finish drawing the parade of
animals and performers as they
head to Madison Square Garden.

MADISON SQUARE GARD

Add a headdress to the collection
at the National Museum of
the American Indian.

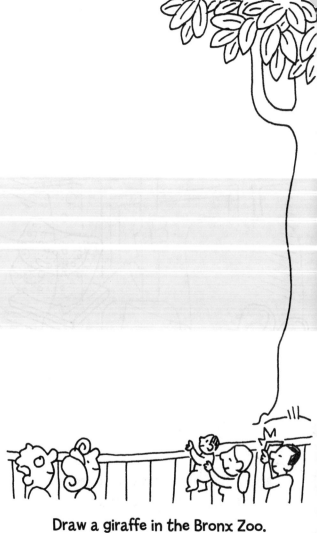

Draw a giraffe in the Bronx Zoo.

What are these subway riders thinking?

Add another dolphin or two to the pool at the New York Aquarium in Brooklyn.

Draw the kids racing on these skates, skateboards and kick scooters to get to school on time.

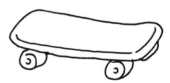

Someone just threw their cell phone
out the window. Finish this drawing.

Design an exhibit for the Children's Museum of Manhattan.

People watching from a sidewalk café. Draw some passersby.

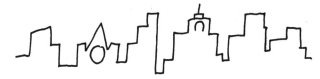

A typical backpack for a New York student holds all these things.

What music are they listening to?

What are these people waiting for a subway train thinking?

Draw a spectacular Christmas
window display for this Fifth
Avenue department store.

The two lion statues that sit in front of the main branch of the New York Public Library at Fifth Avenue and Forty-second Street are named Patience and Fortitude.

Decorate them with some fun designs.

Draw a new crown for the Statue of Liberty.

Draw a figure eight for this ice skater in Prospect Park.

Draw someone you saw on Wall Street.

What are these people on the Cyclone coaster ride in Coney Island screaming?

Draw a postcard from New York.

Draw some beautiful, colorful flowers
for the Brooklyn Botanic Garden.

Add some butterflies to the Butterfly Gardens at the New York Botanical Garden in the Bronx.

Which of these spectators caught a foul ball at Citi Field, home of the New York Mets? Fill in the few blank faces.

Decorate the side of the bus with some ads.

What are these busy New Yorkers thinking?

Connect the lines to complete this drawing.

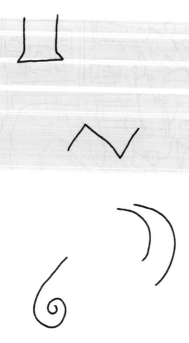

Decorate the Charging Bull statue in
Bowling Green Park near Wall Street.

Design a new MetroCard
for the subway.

Add some dancing water to the fountain
at Lincoln Center for the Performing Arts.

A souvenir page. Paste in memorabilia from your trip to New York—ticket stubs, museum buttons, theatre playbills and other fun stuff.

Design a new playground for Central Park.

Your Observations. Doodle or write about New York traffic.

You're preparing the best pizza in Brooklyn. What's on your pie?

Doodle some toy boats sailing on the famed sailing pond in Central Park's Conservatory Water.

Draw some ice skaters on
Wollman Rink in Central Park.

Doodle a Santa Claus outside Macy's collecting donations for the Salvation Army.

What are this police officer and boy in Times Square saying?

See how many feet you can add to the dragon parading through Chinatown on Chinese New Year.

Design a New York souvenir.

Design a new logo for New York
to complement graphic designer
Milton Glaser's famous I♡NY.

After a Broadway show you wait outside the stage door. Draw the star you'd like to sign your autograph book.

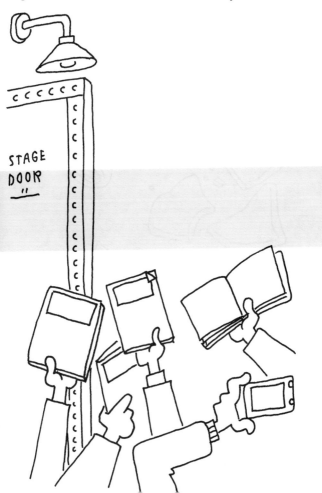

STAGE DOOR

Fortune cookies from a Chinatown restaurant. What does your fortune say?

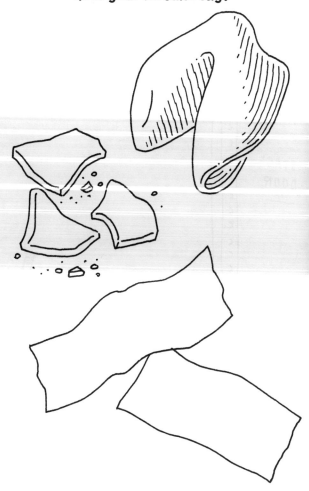

Musicians play music for tips
on the street corner.
Who's playing the instruments?

Design some ads for this subway car.

What message did the plane skywrite over New York?

Hmmm . . . some empty shoes.
Finish this drawing.

A New York Yankees fan and a New York Mets fan debate which is the better team. What are they saying?

Finish drawing the faces of
these New Yorkers.

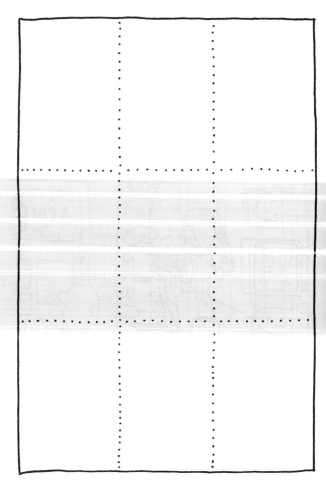

Create a commemorative stamp
series featuring New York.

Draw someone you saw in Harlem.

Create a new ride at Coney Island.

There's a new exhibit on doodles at an art gallery on Madison Avenue.

The wall is your canvas—go for it!

Draw this New Yorker's new tattoo.

Create some weird hairdos for these New Yorkers.

What are these people protesting outside the United Nations?

Draw the famous illuminated Waterford Crystal ball dropping at midnight in Times Square on New Year's Eve.

Doodle the advertising billboards on the tops of these yellow cabs.

Connect the lines to complete this drawing.

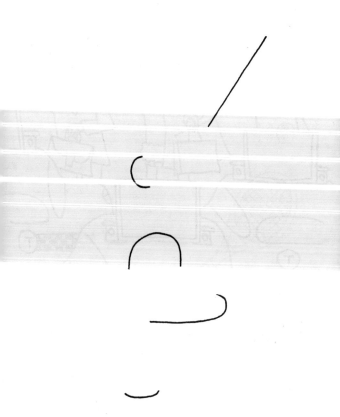

Draw the tennis player about
to return this smash at the U.S.
Open Championship at Flushing
Meadows-Corona Park in Queens.

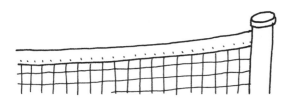

Draw this very pampered pet about to dine on its evening meal.

What is this interesting group of subway riders saying and thinking?

She's spied a rat on the subway tracks. Draw it!

What are these Mexican mariachi players in the subway singing?

What's that conversation you overhear in a fancy restaurant?

Draw a muscleman showing off at Brighton Beach.

What's creeping out of the manhole?

A zombie is auditioning for a part in a Broadway musical.

Your Observations. Doodle or write about eating in New York.

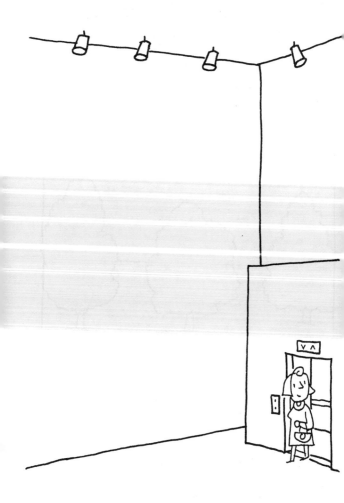

Fill the walls with artwork at
this art gallery in Chelsea.

What movie are you seeing at the Open Air Film Festival at Bryant Park on Forty-second Street?

Describe something funny that happened while you were in New York.

Fishing in the Hudson River. What has this lucky fisherman just caught?

New Yorkers wait "on line," not "in line."

What could these people be thinking about as they wait?

Draw some of the gourmet food
this shopper bought at Zabar's.

For whom are these limousine drivers holding up signs at the airport?

Draw the unique shoes these women are looking at through the window of this boutique.

Decorate the Empire State Building for Valentine's Day.

Draw someone you saw in the East Village.

A young couple is taking wedding pictures at the Conservatory Garden in Central Park. Finish this photo.

Draw the balloons this girl's father bought her at the Bronx Zoo.

Draw the city skyline behind
it as this Circle Line boat
cruises around Manhattan.

This man's ordering a hot dog from a street vendor. What's he telling the vendor to put on his dog?

This giant squirrel and little boy
have found some acorns in the
park. What are they saying?

This dog won top prize at the Westminister Kennel Club Dog Show. Draw it!

Doodle a mosaic panel for the Times Square subway station.

You've discovered a trendy new store in SoHo. What's displayed in its window?

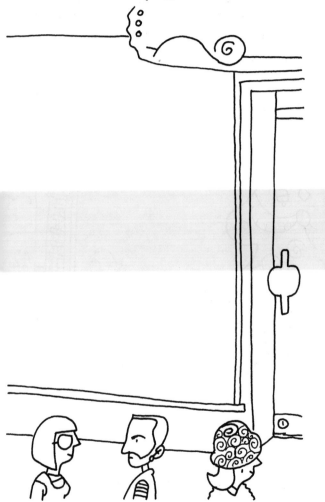

Draw a dancer in the annual
Nutcracker ballet at Lincoln Center.

Draw the dogs this dog walker
is being paid to walk.

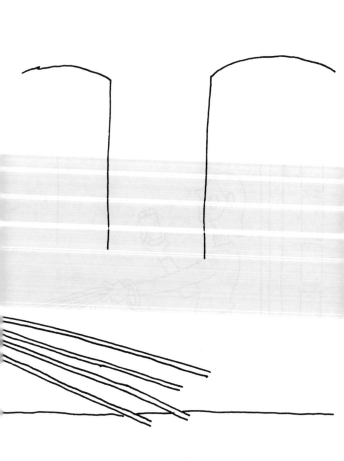

Write down an adventure you had in the Big Apple.

Add some more levels to the Solomon R. Guggenheim Museum building.

Design a pattern for a New York City necktie.

Add some flowerpots to the fire escape in this tenement.

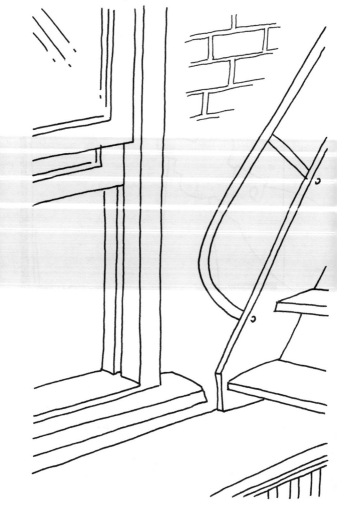

Artist Jackson Pollock was famous for creating paintings by dripping and splattering paint on his canvases. Fill in the canvas of this Pollock "drip" painting at the Museum of Modern Art.

Alien spaceships above New York City!
What messages are they broadcasting?

This diva is making her debut in *La Traviata* at the Metropolitan Opera. Fill in the background behind her.

This girl is wearing a crown like the Statue of Liberty's. Draw it.

What are they planting in Gramercy Park?

What's this juggler at the South Street Seaport juggling?

Finish this drawing.

Finish this totem pole for the National Museum of the American Indian.

What's the best thing
about the Big Apple?

What's the worst thing
about the Big Apple?

Draw some seals at the
Central Park Zoo.

Draw some stars on the Sky Ceiling in the Main Concourse of Grand Central Terminal.

Doodle a gargoyle on the parapet of this apartment house on Central Park West.

Sunbathing on the Great Lawn in Central Park. What is this couple saying?

Draw someone you saw on the Upper East Side.

Draw your great-great-great-ancestor arriving by ship at Ellis Island.

Saturday afternoon playing bongos in Central Park. Draw the bongos.

It's rappers night in New York.
What are they rapping?

Connect the lines to complete this drawing.

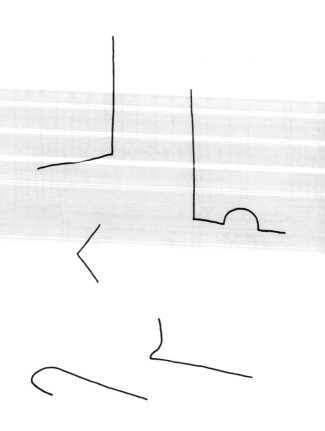

There are some very old gravestones
in the cemetery of Trinity Church
in the downtown financial district.
What inscriptions are on these?

These two kids are playing checkers in the park. What are they saying?

Draw two sweethearts meeting at the clock at the main information booth in Grand Central Terminal.

What do all these different signs say?

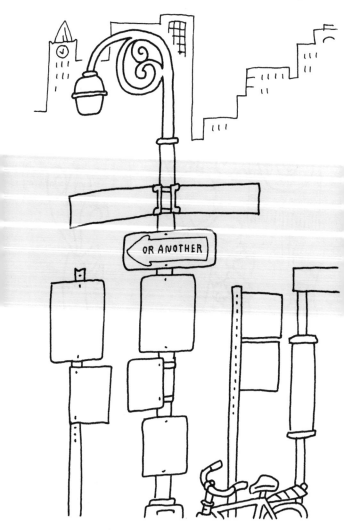

Mounted knights joust each year
at the Medieval Festival held near
the Cloisters in Fort Tryon Park.

Add some designs to the pennants, shields, and helmets; and don't forget the cloth caparisons draped over the horses!

What is this woman thinking
as she waits for a bus?

Doodle the winner of the New York City Marathon crossing the finish line.

What does this grandmother see out the window of her apartment building?

Create a menu for a great New York Sunday morning brunch.

What great treasure have you
discovered at the Sunday flea
market on the Upper West Side?

Your Observations. Doodle or write about the New York art scene.

What's in the New York hero sandwich this man's dreaming of?

The High Line is a unique public park on the West Side built on an old elevated rail line. Doodle a view of Manhattan from this vantage point.

She's radically changed her fashion style since coming to New York! Draw her hair and clothes before . . .

. . . and after.

Who's playing music at the Naumburg Bandshell in Central Park?

What is the train conductor saying as the train pulls away from the station?

It's a New York baby boom!
Decorate these baby strollers.

The streets of New York are filled with interesting characters. Draw a parrot on this girl's shoulder and write what they're saying to each other!

Doodle the dirigible (airship) flying over the Manhattan skyline.

It's summer and the sprinklers are
working in the children's playground.
Draw yourself getting soaked!

What's he saying on his cell phone?
And what's she thinking?

You've made a new best friend in
New York. Describe him or her.

This crowd of protestors is unhappy about something. What do their signs say?

What are they looking at?

What is this sidewalk chalk
artist drawing?

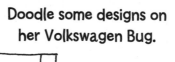

Doodle some designs on her Volkswagen Bug.

Playing hopscotch in Brooklyn. Draw the hopscotch pattern on the ground.

What's this taxi driver saying to his passenger in the back seat?

Have you seen any celebrities in
New York? List them, draw them
or paste their photos here.

You made a great discovery
in an East Side thrift store.
What did you find there?

Draw someone you saw in Central Park.

Draw yourself practicing Tai Chi in Chinatown with these people.

Who's sitting in the window at this coffee shop?

You found an ultracool action figure at the Forbidden Planet comic store. Draw it!

How does a tourist look? How does a New Yorker look? Draw them.

Connect the lines to complete this drawing.

Draw the kite that got caught in this tree in Prospect Park in Brooklyn.

Design your own special yoga pose.

Your Observations. Doodle or write about your favorite Broadway show.

What's this doorman thinking?

There's an important sale at Sotheby's auction house. Draw the painting or object being sold.

Someone's handed you a flyer while you were walking along the street. What's it say?

Draw this animal waiting to be adopted at the Humane Society of New York.

What was the best meal you had while in New York? Draw the restaurant menu.

Is she ordering three lattes, waving at a friend, or hailing a cab? Finish this drawing.

It's raining in New York. Give these soggy folks some umbrellas.

Draw some of the unusual art displayed
at the Outsider Art Fair in Chelsea.

A human billboard on the streets
of New York. What is he selling?

Draw some ads on this subway platform.

A bike messenger is about to collide with a woman texting on her cell phone. What's he yelling? What's she thinking?

This Times Square portrait artist is drawing you. Finish his drawing.

Connect the lines to complete this drawing.

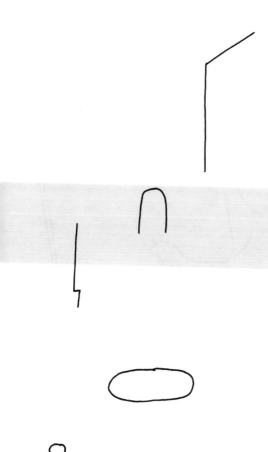

Draw the cartoon characters posing
for pictures with you in Times Square.

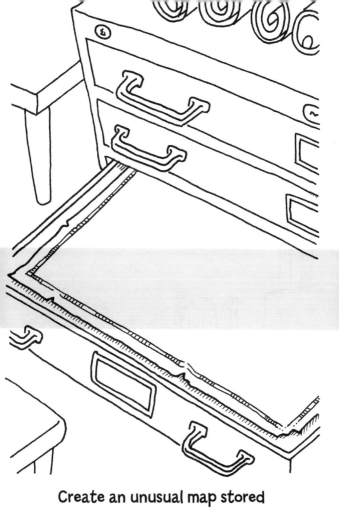

Create an unusual map stored
in the famed map room of the
New York Public Library.

Draw some of the fruits and
vegetables being delivered to the
Union Square Greenmarket.

This woman on Sixth Avenue dressed as the Statue of Liberty is drawing a crowd. What's she thinking? And what's the man walking by thinking?

Draw someone you saw on the Upper West Side.

Design some unique buttons
to be sold at the tiny Tender
Buttons shop in Manhattan.

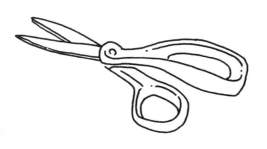

Who's the most interesting person you met in New York?

Add some rock sculptures to the garden of the Noguchi Museum in Long Island City.

Draw the gorgeous necklace you purchased in New York's Diamond District.

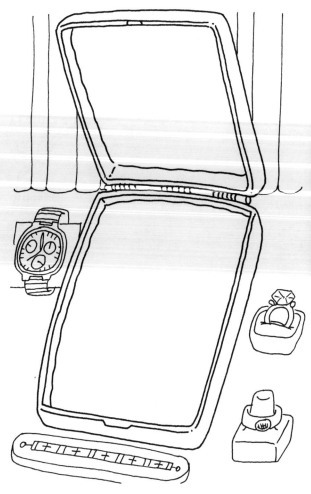

They're digging under the streets of Manhattan. What do they see?

A joyful family reunion. What are these family members saying?

Backed into a corner!
Finish this drawing.

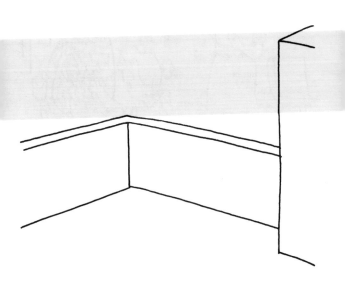

Finish this painting purchased at the Washington Square Outdoor Art Exhibit.

Draw someone you saw in Chelsea.

What's this guitar player in Greenwich Village's Washington Square Park singing?

Your Observations. Doodle or write about the people of New York.

About Bill Zimmerman

Bill Zimmerman has made it his life's work to pioneer interactive techniques that help people tap into their creativity and express themselves through writing and drawing. He has authored nineteen other books, including *Pocketdoodles for Kids*; *Pocketdoodles for Young Artists*; *Doodles and Daydreams: Your Passport for Becoming an Escape Artist*; *Laptop Letters: Sending Wise & Loving Messages to Young People in Your Life*; *Your Life in Comics: 100 Things for Guys to Write and Draw*; *Make Beliefs*; *Lunch Box Letters: Writing Notes of Love and Encouragement to Your Children*; and *100 Things Guys Need to Know*.

Visit Bill's Web sites:
www.MakeBeliefsComix.com
www.billztreasurechest.com
www.facebook.com/MakeBeliefs

About Tom Bloom

Tom Bloom has brought joy to the world with his cartoons and illustrations, which have appeared in many publications, including the *New York Times*, *The New Yorker*, *Fortune*, and *Barron's*.

Share with Us!

We welcome your feedback about this book. What do you like to draw? What else would you like to see? Please send us your suggestions on how we can improve this book, along with your permission to use your ideas in future printings. For every idea used, a free copy of one of our doodling books will be sent to you.

Send your comments to:
Bill Zimmerman
MakeBeliefsComix.com
201 West 77 Street, Suite 6A
New York, NY 10024
billz@makebeliefscomix.com

Also by Bill Zimmerman and Tom Bloom

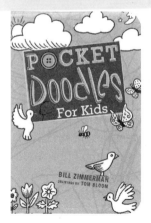